The Ultimate Ramen Cookbook

Over 25 Ramen Noodle Recipes

The Only Ramen Noodle Cookbook You Will Ever Need

BY

Rachael Rayner

Copyright 2016 Rachael Rayner

License Notes

No part of this Book can be reproduced in any form or by any means including print, electronic, scanning or photocopying unless prior permission is granted by the author.

All ideas, suggestions and guidelines mentioned here are written for informative purposes. While the author has taken every possible step to ensure accuracy, all readers are advised to follow information at their own risk. The author cannot be held responsible for personal and/or commercial damages in case of misinterpreting and misunderstanding any part of this Book

For a complete list of my published books, please, visit my Author's Page:

https://www.amazon.com/author/rachael.rayner

Table of Contents

Introduction 5
Delicious Ramen Cooker Recipes 7
- Easy Cheeseburger Ramen Casserole 8
- Thai Style Chicken Ramen 10
- Classic Dragon Noodles 12
- Lime and Shrimp Dragon Noodles 15
- Ramen Noodle Taco Bowls 17
- Ramen Noodle Chicken Stir Fry Smothered in Peanut Sauce 19
- Spicy Macaroni and Cheese Ramen Noodle 22
- Mongolian Style Beef Ramen Noodles 24
- Simple Garlic Noodles 26
- Easy Creamy Ramen Noodles 28
- Easy Ramen Noodle Casserole 30
- Simple Chicken Chow Mein 32
- Oriental Style Ramen Coleslaw 34
- Sesame Style Peanut Butter Noodles 36
- Amazing Asian Ramen Salad 38
- Cantonese Style Noodles 40
- Sausage and Ramen Noodle Stir Fry 42
- Black Chicken Ramen Noodle Soup 44
- 20 Minute Shrimp and Sriracha Ramen 47
- Classic Beef and Broccoli Noodle Bowls 50
- Cheesy Italian Baked Ramen Noodles 54

Simple Sesame Noodles 56

Taco Style Ramen Bowls 58

Pot Sticker Noodle Bowls 60

Beef Pho Noodle Soup 62

Conclusion 64

Author's Afterthoughts 65

About The Author 66

Introduction

Known in Japan as menrui, ramen noodles are not only a significant food source in Japan, but they have become one in the states as well. Depending on where you visit the flavor of ramen with vary greatly and some people will swear to consume only certain flavors. There are many different ways that you can adapt ramen noodles to your own flavor and to make dishes that are truly delicious.

If you are a huge fan of ramen noodles and have wanted to make your own ramen noodle dishes, then this is the perfect dish for you to enjoy. Inside of this book you will learn how to make your own ramen dishes by discovering over 25 of the most delicious ramen noodle recipes you have ever come across. Remember, each recipe that you find in this can be adapted to fit your specific tastes and preferences.

So, without further ado, let's get cooking!

Delicious Ramen Cooker Recipes

Easy Cheeseburger Ramen Casserole

Here is a simple and delicious way to transform your future ramen noodle dishes. It turns even the most boring ramen dishes into a meal the entire family won't soon forget.

Makes: 4 Servings

Total Prep Time: 30 Minutes

Ingredients:

- 1 ½ Pounds of Beef, Lean and Ground
- 1 Cup of Onions, Finely Chopped
- 3, 3 Ounce Packs of Ramen Noodles, Beef Flavored
- 2 Cups of Water, Warm
- ¾ Cup of Ketchup
- 1 Tbsp. of Mustard, Yellow in Color
- ¼ Cup of Relish, Sweet Pickle Variety
- 2 Cups of Cheddar Cheese, Finely Shredded

Directions:

1. The first thing that you will want to do is preheat your oven to 350 degrees. While your oven is heating up grease a large sized baking dish with some cooking spray.

2. Then use a large sized skillet and place over high heat. Once your skillet is hot enough add in your beef and onions. Cook for the next 6 to 8 minutes or until your beef is fully browned.

3. Add in your water and seasoning packets and stir to combine.

4. Bring this mixture to a boil.

5. Once your mixture is boiling add in your noodles and continue to cook for the next 3 minutes or until your noodles are soft to the touch.

6. Remove from heat and add in your ketchup, sweet relish and yellow mustard. Stir to combine.

7. Pour your mixture into your greased baking dish and place into your oven to bake for the next 20 to 25 minutes.

8. Remove and allow to cool slightly before serving.

Thai Style Chicken Ramen

This is a great tasting ramen recipe to make if you are looking for something on the spicy side. It is easy to make and makes for the perfect filling dish to enjoy any day of the week.

Makes: 4 Servings

Total Prep Time: 12 Minutes

Ingredients:

- 1 Tbsp. of Oil, Vegetable Variety
- 1 Red Bell Pepper, Sliced Into Thin Strips
- 1 Cup of Carrots, Matchstick Variety
- 4 Green Onions, Evenly Divided and Thinly Sliced
- 1 Tbsp. of Green Curry Paste, Thai Variety
- 4 Cups of Water, Warm
- 1, 14 Ounce Can of Milk, Coconut Variety and Light
- 1 Tbsp. of Fish Sauce
- 2, 3.5 Ounce Cans of Flavoring, Tonkotsu Variety
- 10 Ounces of Chicken Breast, Fully Cooked and Shredded
- 1 Tbsp. of Lime Juice, Fresh
- ½ Cup of Cilantro, Fresh, Roughly Chopped and Evenly Divided
- Dash of Sesame Seeds, Lightly Toasted and For Garnish

Directions:

1. First heat up some oil in a large sized pot placed over medium to high heat. Once your oil is hot enough add in your bell peppers, fresh carrots and half of your green onions. Cook for at least one mine before adding in your curry paste.

2. Continue to cook for an additional minute. Then add in your water, coconut milk and fish sauce.

3. Allow your mixture to come to a boil.

4. Once boiling add in your ramen and allow to boil for the next 4 minutes, making sure to stir occasionally.

5. Add your ramen seasoning into a small sized bowl and ladle at least one cup of your cooking liquid into the bowl. Stir to combine and add into your pot.

6. Add in your fresh lime juice, shredded chicken and half of your fresh cilantro. Stir to combine and remove from heat.

7. Divide your mixture among 4 serving bowls. Top off with your remaining cilantro, green onions and sesame seeds. Serve right away and enjoy.

Classic Dragon Noodles

This ramen recipe if packed full of chicken, veggies and shrimp, making it the perfect meal to serve up if you are looking for something on the filling side. It is packed full of bowl flavors, I'm sure everyone will love it.

Makes: 4 Servings

Total Prep Time: 35 Minutes

Ingredients:

- 2 Packs of Ramen Noodles, Plain
- 2 Tbsp. of Sriracha
- 2 Tbsp. of Soy Sauce, Your Favorite Kind
- 2 Tbsp. of Brown Sugar, Light and Packed
- 3 Tbsp. of Olive oil, Extra Virgin Variety
- 2 Eggs, Large in Size and Beaten Lightly
- 6 to 8 Pieces of Shrimp, Large in Size, Peeled and Deveined
- ¼ pound of Chicken Breast, Boneless, Skinless and Thinly Sliced
- ½ of an Onion, Small in Size, Peeled and Finely Chopped
- 2 Cloves of Garlic, Peeled and Minced
- 1 Carrot, Large in Size, Peeled and Cut Julienne Style
- ¼ of a Cabbage, Fresh and Roughly Shredded
- 1 Cup of Bean Sprouts, Fresh

- Some Green Onions, Finely Chopped
- ½ tsp. of Red Pepper Flakes

Directions:

1. In a large sized pot placed over medium heat, add in your ramen noodles and cook according to the directions on the package. Once cooked drain and set aside to keep warm. Make sure that you reserve at least two spoonfuls of the cooking liquid.

2. Then use a small sized bowl add in your reserved cooking liquid, sriracha sauce, favorite soy sauce and light brown sugar. Stir thoroughly to combine and until your sugar is fully dissolved. Set this mixture aside for later use.

3. Use a large sized wok and set over medium heat. Add in your oil and once your oil is hot enough add in your eggs. Cook until fully set and moist. Remove your eggs from your wok and keep warm.

4. Heat up some more oil and add in your shrimp. Cook until your shrimp turns pink in color. Remove from your pan and set aside to keep warm.

5. Heat up some more oil and once your oil is hot enough add in your onions and garlic. Cook until soft to the touch. Then add in your chicken and cook until your chicken is fully cooked through.

6. Add in your carrots and continue to cook until tender to the touch. Add in your cabbage and continue to cook for an additional minute.

7. Add in your cooked noodles, cooked shrimp and your premade sauce. Toss thoroughly to combine. Add in your cooked eggs and fresh bean sprouts. Toss again to combine and continue to cook for an additional 1 to 2 minutes.

8. Remove from heat and serve with a garnish of green onions and red pepper flakes. Enjoy.

Lime and Shrimp Dragon Noodles

Here is yet another dragon noodle dish I know you won't be able to get enough of. It only takes a few ingredients to put together making it perfect for those who are on a tight budget.

Makes: 2 to 4 Servings

Total Prep Time: 15 Minutes

Ingredients:

- ½ Pound of Shrimp, Peeled and Deveined
- 2 Packs of Ramen Noodles, Plain Variety
- 2 Tbsp. of Sriracha
- 2 Tbsp. of Soy Sauce, Your Favorite Kind
- 2 Tbsp. of Brown Sugar, Light and Packed
- 1 Lime, Fresh
- 2 Tbsp. of Butter, Soft
- 2 Cloves of Garlic, Minced
- 2 Green Onions
- 1 Handful of Cilantro

Directions:

1. First place your shrimp into a colander and rinse with some water until completely thawed. Once thawed allow your shrimp to drain until you are ready to use it.

2. Then use a small sized bowl and add in your Sriracha, favorite kind of soy sauce, light brown sugar and at least a spoonful of fresh lime juice. Stir to combine and set aside for later use.

3. Fill up a medium sized sauce pot with some water and bring to a boil over high heat. Once your water is boiling add in your ramen noodles and cook until they are tender to the touch. Once tender drain and set aside for later use.

4. Use a large sized skillet placed over medium heat and add in your butter and garlic. Cook until your garlic is soft to the touch.

5. Then add in your shrimp and continue to cook until your shrimp is pink and opaque. This should take at least 3 to 5 minutes. Remove from heat.

6. Add your cooked noodles to your skillet with your shrimp and pour your sauce over the top. Toss to combine and serve with your green onions and cilantro.

Ramen Noodle Taco Bowls

If you are craving authentic Mexican cuisine, then this is the perfect dish for you to make. This is the perfect dish to make for your average college student and will leave them feeling incredibly satisfied.

Makes: 4 Servings

Total Prep Time: 12 Minutes

Ingredients:

- 1 Pound of Beef, Lean and Ground
- ½ of an Onion, White in Color and Fully Chopped
- 3 Tbsp. of Taco Seasoning
- 2 Packs of Ramen, Plain and with Seasoning Discarded
- 1, 11 Ounce Can of Corn, Whole Kernel Variety and Drained
- 1, 15 Ounce Can of Black Beans, Drained
- 1, 10 Ounce Can of Tomatoes, Rotel Variety
- 1 Handful of Cilantro, Fresh and Roughly Chopped
- Some Tomato, For Serving
- Some Sour Cream, For Serving
- Some Salsa, For Serving
- Some Avocado, For Serving

Directions:

1. The first thing that you will want to do is boil your ramen noodles in a large sized pot until tender to the touch. Once tender drain and set aside for later use.

2. Next use a large sized skillet placed over medium heat to cook your beef until it is brown in color.

3. Add in your onions and taco seasoning and continue to cook for at least 5 minutes.

4. Then add in your tomatoes, whole kernel corn, black beans, fresh cilantro and cooked noodles. Toss to combine and continue to cook until piping hot.

5. Remove from heat and serve with your desired topping.

Ramen Noodle Chicken Stir Fry Smothered in Peanut Sauce

If you are looking for the perfect recipe to serve up to those picky eaters in your household, then this is the perfect dish for you to make. It incredibly healthy and paced full of a flavor nobody will be able to resist.

Makes: 2 Servings

Total Prep Time: 40 Minutes

Ingredients For Your Peanut Sauce:

- ½ Cup of Peanut Butter, Crunchy Variety
- 2 Tbsp. of Soy Sauce, Your Favorite Kind
- 1 Tbsp. of Sugar, White in Color
- 2 Drops of Hot Pepper Sauce, Your Favorite Kind
- 1 Clove of Garlic, Minced
- ½ Cup of Water, Warm

Ingredients For Your Stir Fry:

- 2 Tbsp. of Oil, Peanut Variety
- 1 Chicken Breast, Boneless and Cut Into Small Sized Cubes
- 1, 3 Ounce Pack of Ramen Noodles, Plain
- ¾ Cup of Red Bell Peppers, Finely Diced
- ¾ Cup of Yellow Onion, Finely Diced
- 1 Cup of Carrots, Baby Variety and Sliced In Halves
- 2 Cups of Broccoli, Cut Into Florets

Directions:

1. The first thing that you will want to do is make your peanut sauce. To do this use a large sized bowl and add in all of your ingredients for your peanut sauce into it. Stir thorough to combine and set aside for later use.

2. Place your chicken into your peanut sauce and allow to marinate for at least 15 minutes.

3. After this time place your marinated chicken into a small sized pan placed over medium heat. Cook for at least 10 to 15 minutes or until completely cooked thorough.

4. Next cook your ramen noodles according to the directions on the package or until fully cooked. Once cooked coat in your peanut sauce and set aside.

5. Use a large sized skillet and heat up your peanut oil. Once your oil is hot enough add in your bell peppers, carrots, onions and broccoli florets. Cook for at least 10 minutes or until your veggies are soft to the touch.

6. Then add in your cooked chicken and cooked noodles. Toss to coat and cook for another 5 minutes.

7. Remove from heat and enjoy while still piping hot.

Spicy Macaroni and Cheese Ramen Noodle

If you are a huge fan of macaroni and cheese, then this is the perfect dish for you to enjoy. Smothered in delicious cheese, this is one dish you are going to want to make if you are looking to spoil yourself.

Makes: 2 Servings

Total Prep Time: 12 Minutes

Ingredients:

- 4, 3 Ounce Packs of Ramen Noodles, Noodles Only
- 1 Tbsp. of Butter, Soft
- 1 Tbsp. of Flour, All Purpose Variety
- 1 ½ Cups of Milk, Whole
- 1, 8 Ounce Pack of Cheese, Pepper Jack Variety and Finely Shredded
- 2 tsp. of Sriracha Sauce
- ½ tsp. of Salt, For Taste

Directions:

1. First bring a large sized pot of water to a boil and add in your noodles. Boil your noodles until they are tender to the touch. Remove and drain.

2. Toss your noodles with some oil and set aside for later use.

3. Heat up some butter in a large sized saucepan placed over medium heat. Add in your flour and whisk thoroughly to form a roux. Cook for at least one minute.

4. Add in your milk and continue to cook until your mixture becomes thick in consistency.

5. Reduce the heat to low and slowly add in your cheese. Add in your Sriracha and dash of salt. Stir to combine and continue to stir until your cheese is fully melted.

6. Increase the heat to medium and add in your noodles. Toss to combine and continue to cook for an additional minute or two.

7. Remove from heat and serve while still piping hot.

Mongolian Style Beef Ramen Noodles

This recipe is a popular restaurant copycat recipe that I know you will fall in love with, especially if you are a huge fan of classic Chinese food. It is incredibly simple to make and makes for a meal you won't soon forget.

Makes: 4 Servings

Total Prep Time: 50 Minutes

Ingredients:

- 1 ½ Pound of Flank Steak
- ¼ Cup of Cornstarch
- ¼ Cup of Oil, Vegetable Variety
- 1 Green Bell Pepper, Sliced Into Thin Strips
- 8 Ounces of Ramen Noodles, Dried
- 3 Green Onions, Finely Chopped

Ingredients For Your Sauce:

- 2 Tbsp. of Oil, Sesame Variety
- ¾ Cup of Soy Sauce, Your Favorite Kind
- 2/3 Cup of Brown Sugar, Light and Packed
- 1 ¼ Cup of Chicken Broth, Homemade Preferable
- 4 Cloves of Garlic, Minced
- ¼ tsp. of Red Pepper Flakes

Directions:

1. Add your flank steak into a large sized Ziploc bag along with your cornstarch. Seal the bad and toss to coat.

2. Then use a large sized skillet and add in your oil. Set over medium heat and once your oil is hot enough add in your beef and cook until brown in color. Remove from your skillet and set aside for later use.

3. Add your bell peppers into your skillet and cook until soft to the touch. Remove from your skillet and set aside for later use.

4. Using the same skillet add in all of your ingredients for your sauce. Stir to thoroughly combine and cook for the next 10 minutes or until your sauce is thick in consistency.

5. While your sauce is cooking, cook your noodles according to the directions on the package or until your noodles are soft to the touch. Once tender drain and add to your skillet with your sauce.

6. Add in your beef and cooked bell peppers to your skillet and toss to combine. Cook for an additional minute or until piping hot.

7. Remove from heat and serve with a garnish of green onions.

Simple Garlic Noodles

Here is yet another budget friendly ramen recipe that you won't be able to resist. It is simple to make and makes for a filling meal that you will want to enjoy over and over again.

Makes: 4 Servings

Total Prep Time: 25 Minutes

Ingredients:

- 8 Ounces of Pasta, Angel Hair Variety
- 4 Cloves of Garlic, Minced
- ½ Bunch of Green Onions, Fresh
- 4 Tbsp. of Butter, Soft
- 2 tsp. of Soy Sauce, Your Favorite Kind
- 2 Tbsp. of Brown Sugar, Light and Packed
- 1 tsp. of Oil, Sesame Variety
- 2 Tbsp. of Oyster Sauce

Directions:

1. Add your oyster sauce, light brown sugar, favorite soy sauce and oil into a large sized bowl. Stir thoroughly to combine.

2. Then bring a large sized pot of water to a boil and cook your pasta according to the directions on the package or until tender to the touch. Drain and set aside for later use.

3. Add some butter into a large sized skillet and place over low to medium heat. Once your butter is fully melted add in your onions and garlic and cook for at least 1 to 2 minutes or until they are fragrant.

4. Remove your skillet from heat and add in your drained pasta and oyster sauce. Stir well to coat.

5. Serve with a garnish of green onions and enjoy immediately.

Easy Creamy Ramen Noodles

This is a kid friendly ramen noodle recipe that every kid will fall in love with. It makes for a great tasting meal or as an easy side dish to go along with any elegant entrée that you may make.

Makes: 2 Servings

Total Prep Time: 10 Minutes

Ingredients:

- 1, 3 Ounce Pack of Ramen, Any Flavor
- 2 Cups of Water, Warm
- 2 Tbsp. of Butter, Soft
- ¼ Cup of Milk, Whole

Directions:

1. First bring some water to a boil in a small sized saucepan.

2. Once your water is boiling add in your noodles and cook for at least 3 minutes or until your noodles are tender to the touch. Make sure that you stir occasionally.

3. Once tender remove and drain. Return your noodles back into your pot.

4. Heat over low heat and add in your butter and milk. Stir thoroughly to coat.

5. Remove from heat and serve right away.

Easy Ramen Noodle Casserole

Here is a simple ramen recipe that you can put together when you need to through dinner together last minute. Serve this with a fresh salad to make a meal you won't soon forget.

Makes: 6 t0 8 Servings

Total Prep Time: 25 Minutes

Ingredients:

- 1 Pound of Chuck, Lean and Ground
- 1 Onion, Medium in Size and Finely Diced
- 1, 14.5 Ounce Can of Tomatoes, Finely Diced
- 3, 3 Ounce Pack of Ramen Noodles, Beef Flavored
- 3 Cups of Water, Warm
- Some Velveeta Cheese

Directions:

1. The first thing that you will want to do is place your chuck and onion into a large sized skillet placed over medium heat. Cook for the next 5 to 10 minutes or until brown in color.

2. Add your flavor packets from your noodles and allow to simmer for the next 4 minutes.

3. Add in your water and tomatoes. Bring this mixture to a boil.

4. Add in your ramen noodles and continue to cook for the next 4 minutes.

5. Remove from heat and transfer your mixture into a large sized casserole dish. Cover with your Velveeta cheese.

6. Place into your oven to bake for the next 15 minutes at 350 degrees or until your cheese is fully melted.

7. Remove and allow to cool slightly before serving.

Simple Chicken Chow Mein

Here is yet another ramen noodle recipe that I know you are going to fall in love with. It is packed full of flavor and makes for a great tasting meal for those who are on a tight budget.

Makes: 3 to 4 Servings

Total Prep Time: 20 Minutes

Ingredients:

- 2, 3 Ounce Packs of Ramen Noodles, Seasoning Packets Discarded
- 1 Yellow Onion, Medium in Size and Finely Diced
- 2 Carrots, Medium in Size, Peeled and Finely Diced
- 1 Broccoli, Crown Variety and Cut Into Small Sized Pieces
- ½ Cup of Sugar Snap Peas, Fresh
- 2 Chicken Breasts, Cut Into Small Sized Strips
- 1 Clove of Garlic, Finely Chopped
- 2 Tbsp. of Olive Oil, Extra Virgin Variety
- 1 tsp. of Oil, Sesame Variety
- ¼ Cup of Soy Sauce, Your Favorite Kind
- 3 Tbsp. of Worcestershire Sauce
- 2 Tbsp. of Ketchup, Your Favorite Kind
- 1 Tbsp. of Sriracha
- 1 Tbsp. of Sugar

Directions:

1. Add in your oil into a large sized skillet and set over medium heat. Once your oil is hot enough add in your garlic and cook until soft to the touch.

2. Add in your chicken and cook until brown in color.

3. While your chicken is cooking, cook your ramen noodles according to the directions on the package. Once tender to the touch drain your noodles and set aside from later use. Remove your brown chicken from your skillet.

4. Using the same skillet, add in some more oil and add in your broccoli, carrots and sugar snap peas. Cook for the next 10 minutes or until your veggies are tender to the touch.

5. The use a medium sized bowl and add in your sesame oil, favorite kind of soy sauce, favorite ketchup, Worcestershire sauce, white sugar and Sriracha. Stir thoroughly to combine and pour into your skillet with your tender veggies.

6. Add in your chicken and cooked noodles into your skillet and toss to coat. Cook for at least 1 to 2 minutes, making sure to stir constantly.

7. Remove from heat and serve while still piping hot.

Oriental Style Ramen Coleslaw

Here is an easy and tasty salad recipe that you can make whenever you are craving something on the healthy side. Perfect for any potluck you may attend, once your friends and family get a taste of it I know they won't be able to get enough of it.

Makes: 6 Servings

Total Prep Time: 10 Minutes

Ingredients:

- 1, 14 to 16 Ounce Package of Coleslaw Mix
- 1 Bunch of Green Onions, Sliced Thinly
- ½ Cup of Almonds, Lightly Toasted and Cut Into Slivers
- ½ Cup of Sunflower Seeds
- 1, 3 Ounce Pack of Ramen Noodles, Chicken Flavored
- ½ Cup of Oil, Sunflower Variety
- 1/3 Cup of Vinegar, Cider Variety
- 2 tsp. of Brown Sugar, Light and Packed

Directions:

1. First use a large sized bowl and add in your coleslaw mix, sunflower seeds, fresh green onions and slivered almonds. Stir thoroughly to combine.

2. Then break half of your ramen noodles into small sized pieces and set aside for later use.

3. Use a small sized bowl and add in your oil, vinegar, ramen seasoning packet and sugar. Stir thoroughly until smooth in consistency.

4. Pour your oil on top of your freshly made salad and top off with your ramen pieces. Toss thoroughly to coat.

5. Serve with a garnish of green onions and enjoy.

Sesame Style Peanut Butter Noodles

If you are a huge fan of noodles and peanut butter, then this is one dish you need to try for yourself. It can be made in just a matter of minutes, making it perfect for those who are tight on time.

Makes: 3 Servings

Total Prep Time: 9 Minutes

Ingredients:

- 6 Ounces of Asian Style Noodles
- 2 Tbsp. of Oil, Sesame Variety and Pure
- 1 ½ Tbsp. of Peanut Butter, Smooth Variety
- 2 Tbsp. of Honey, Raw
- 2 Tbsp. of Soy Sauce, Your Favorite Kind
- 1 ½ Tbsp. of Vinegar, Rice Variety
- 1 Clove of Garlic, Minced
- ½ tsp. of Ginger Root, Freshly Grated
- 3 Green Onions, Finely Sliced and For Garnish

Directions:

1. The first thing that you will want to do is cook your noodles according to the directions on the package.

2. Then use a medium sized bowl and add in your smooth peanut butter, raw honey, favorite soy sauce, sesame oil, vinegar, garlic and ginger. Whisk until thoroughly combined.

3. Pour your sauce over your hot cooked noodles and toss thoroughly to coat.

4. Top off with your green onions as a garnish and enjoy.

Amazing Asian Ramen Salad

This ridiculously amazing Asian style ramen salad is one that your friends and family are going to be begging you for the recipe. It is so delicious you will need to make it for your family over and over again.

Makes: 8 to 10 Servings

Total Prep Time: 2 Hours and 10 Minutes

Ingredients:

- 1, 16 Ounce Bag of Coleslaw, Fresh
- 1 Cup of Sunflower Seeds, De-Shelled Variety
- 1 Cup of Almonds, Cut Into Slivers
- 2, 3 Ounce Packs of Ramen, Any Flavor
- 5 Stalks of Scallions, Thinly Sliced
- ¾ Cup of Oil, Vegetable Variety
- 1/3 Cup of Vinegar, White in Color
- ½ Cup of Sugar, Granulated Variety

Directions:

1. Use a large sized bowl and add in your coleslaw mix, sunflower seeds, sliced almonds and ramen. Add in your scallions and toss to combine.

2. Then use a separate medium sized bowl and add in your oil, vinegar and sugar. Whisk until thoroughly combine and pour over your coleslaw mixture. Toss thoroughly to coat

3. Wrap your bowl with some plastic wrap and place into your fridge to chill for the next 2 hours. After this time serve whenever you are ready and enjoy.

Cantonese Style Noodles

Here is yet another ramen recipe that you can make whenever you wish to spoil yourself. It is a great dish to make that comes together in little time.

Makes: 4 to 6 Servings

Total Prep Time: 30 Minutes

Ingredients:

- 12 Ounces of Egg Noodles, Hong Kong Style
- 8 Scallions
- 2 tsp. of Oyster Sauce
- ¼ Cup of Soy Sauce, Low in Sodium
- 2 tsp. of Sugar, White in Color
- 2 tsp. of Garlic, Minced
- ¼ to ½ tsp. of Red Pepper Flakes
- ½ tsp. of Salt, For Taste
- 2 Tbsp. + 2 tsp. of Oil, Sesame Variety and Lightly toasted
- 2 Tbsp. of Oil, Canola Variety
- 1 ½ Cups of Mixed Veggies, Your Favorite Kind

Directions:

1. The first thing that you will want to do is bring a large sized stock pot of water to a boil over medium heat. Once

your water is boiling place your scallions into a separate bowl and set aside for later use.

2. Then use a separate medium sized bowl and add in your oyster sauce, soy sauce, sugar, garlic, pepper flakes, dash of salt and one spoonful of your sesame oil. Stir thoroughly to combine and set aside for later use.

3. Once your water is boiling, add in your noodles and allow them to boil for at least 2 to 4 minutes or until tender to the touch. Once tender, drain and set aside for later use.

4. Heat up a large sized wok over high heat. Once your skillet is hot enough add in your sesame oil and canola oil. Allow your oil to shimmer then add in your noodles in a thin layer. Allow to cook for the next 4 to 6 minutes or until crispy. Flip and continue cooking for an additional 3 minutes. Transfer to a plate.

5. Heat up your remaining sesame oil and add in your scallions. Allow to cook for a couple of seconds before adding your noodles back into your wok. Toss to combine.

6. Add in your mixed veggie mix and slowly add in your soy sauce mixture. Continue to cook for the next 1 to 2 minutes before remove from heat.

7. Add in your bean sprouts and toss to combine. Serve right away and enjoy.

Sausage and Ramen Noodle Stir Fry

If you are looking for a great tasting lunch or dinner recipe to make, then this is the perfect recipe for you. It is incredibly savory and will leave you feeling satisfied all day long.

Makes: 4 Servings

Total Prep Time: 25 Minutes

Ingredients:

- 6 ½ Ounces of Turkey Sausage, Smoked Variety and Thinly Sliced
- 1, 3 Ounce Pack of Ramen Noodle Soup Mix, Any Flavor
- ½ Pound of Snow Peas, Fresh and Trimmed
- 2 Cloves of Garlic, Minced
- 4 Green Onions, Fresh, Thinly Sliced and Evenly Divided
- ¼ Cup of Asian Sesame Dressing, Lightly Toasted

Directions:

1. The first thing that you will want to do is cook your sausage. To do this use a large sized skillet and set over medium to high heat. Once hot enough add in your sausage and cook for the next 5 minutes or until light brown in color. Make sure that you stir occasionally.

2. Discard the seasoning packed from your ramen noodles.

3. Add your noodles to a large sized saucepan and cover with some boil. Allow your noodles to boil for the next 5 minutes or until tender. Once tender drain.

4. Add your snow peas, garlic and half of your onions to your cooked sausage mixture. Cook for an additional 2 to 3 minutes or until your peas are crispy to the touch.

5. Add in your cooked noodles and dressing. Heat again for another 2 minutes.

6. Remove from heat and top off with your remaining onions. Enjoy right away.

Black Chicken Ramen Noodle Soup

This hearty soup is one that I know you will want to make whenever you are feeling a bit under the weather. It is packed full of wholesome carrots and savory ramen noodles; its taste alone will leave you coming back for more.

Makes: 1 Serving

Total Prep Time: 45 Minutes

Ingredients For Your Chicken:

- 1 Pound of Chicken Breasts, Skinless and Boneless Variety
- 2 Tbsp. of Olive Oil, Extra Virgin Variety
- 1 tsp. of Garlic, Powdered Variety
- 1 tsp. of Cumin, Ground
- ½ tsp. of Chili, Powdered Variety
- ½ tsp. of Cayenne Pepper
- ½ tsp. of Oregano, Dried
- ¾ tsp. of Salt, For Taste
- ¾ tsp. of Black Pepper, For Taste

Ingredients For Your Soup:

- 2 Tbsp. of Olive Oil, Extra Virgin Variety
- 2 Tbsp. of Sriracha Sauce
- 1 Onion, Small in Size and Finely Diced
- 2 Tbsp. of Tomato Paste
- 1 Tbsp. of Ginger, Freshly Grated
- 3 Carrots, Peeled and Chopped Into Small Sized Pieces
- 2 Cups of Kale, Fresh and Roughly Chopped
- 5 Cloves of Garlic, Minced
- ½ tsp. of Garlic, Powdered Variety
- ½ tsp. of Salt, Celery Variety
- 4 Cups of Chicken Stock, Homemade Preferable
- 2 Cups of Water, Warm
- 1 Tbsp. of Soy Sauce, Your Favorite Kind
- 1 tsp. of Vinegar, Rice Variety
- 3 Packs of Ramen Noodles, Any Flavor
- ½ Cup of Scallions, Fresh and Finely Chopped

Directions:

1. The first thing that you will want to do is make your chicken. To do this preheat your oven to 375 degrees. Then line a large sized baking dish with some parchment paper.

2. Add your chicken into your baking dish. Drizzle your oil over the top and sprinkle with your cumin, garlic, chili, oregano, cayenne pepper and dash of salt and pepper.

3. Place into your oven to bake for the next 25 minutes, making sure to flip at least once halfway through. Remove and cut your chicken into strips.

4. Next make your soup. To do this add some oil and Sriracha to a large sized stockpot. Bring to a simmer over medium to high heat. Once your stockpot is hot enough add in your onions and tomato paste. Cook for at least 4 minutes, making sure to stir occasionally.

5. Then add in your ginger, garlic, garlic salt and dash of salt and pepper. Cook for an additional 2 minutes or until fragrant.

6. Add in your chicken stock and water and bring your mixture to a boil. Once boiling add in your soy sauce and vinegar. Allow to simmer for an additional 8 to 10 minutes.

7. Add in your remaining ingredients including your noodles and continue to cook for another 2 to 3 minutes.

8. Remove from heat and serve your dish on top of your cooked chicken. Enjoy.

20 Minute Shrimp and Sriracha Ramen

Just as the name implies this is a delicious ramen dish that you can have on your table in 20 minutes or less. It is packed full of spicy flavor, I know you won't be able to get enough of it.

Makes: 6 Servings

Total Prep Time: 20 Minutes

Ingredients:

- 3 Tbsp. of Oil, Sesame Variety and Evenly Divided
- ½ Pound of Shrimp, Peeled and Deveined
- 1 tsp. of Basil, Dried
- ½ tsp. of Salt, For Taste
- ½ tsp. of Black Pepper, For Taste
- 2 Tbsp. of Sriracha
- 1 Onion, Yellow in Color and Finely Diced
- 1 Red Bell Pepper, Finely Diced
- 1 Tbsp. of ginger, Freshly Grated
- 6 Cloves of Garlic, Minced
- 4 Cups of Chicken Stock, Homemade Preferable
- 2 Cups of Water, Warm
- 2 Tbsp. of Tomato Paste
- ½ tsp. of Garlic, Powdered Variety
- ½ tsp. of Onion, Powdered Variety
- ½ tsp. of Salt, Celery Variety

- 1 ½ Tbsp. of Soy Sauce, Your Favorite Kind
- 1 tsp. of Vinegar, Rice Variety
- 3 Packs of Ramen, Any Flavor
- 1 Cup of Spinach, Baby Variety and Chopped Roughly
- 2 Tbsp. of Lemon Juice, Fresh

Directions:

1. Heat up some sesame oil in a large sized soup pot place over medium to high heat. Once your oil is hot enough add in your shrimp and season with a dash of basil, salt and pepper. Cook for at least one minute on each side or until pink in color. Remove and transfer to a cutting board.

2. Using the same soup pot add in your remaining sesame oil. Once your oil is hot enough add in your Sriracha sauce, onions and red bell peppers. Cook for at least 4 minutes or until your onions are soft to the touch.

3. Then add in your ginger and garlic and continue to cook for an additional minute.

4. Add in your chicken stock and water. Stir thoroughly to combine and bring to a boil.

5. Once boiling add in your tomato paste, powdered garlic, powdered onion, salt, favorite soy sauce and vinegar. Stir thoroughly to combine and reduce the heat to low. Allow to simmer for the next 8 minutes.

6. Add in your ramen noodles to your broth and continue to cook for 2 more minutes.

7. Add in your chopped shrimp, spinach and fresh lemon juice. Cook for another 4 minutes or until your spinach begins to wilt.

8. Remove from heat and serve while still piping hot.

Classic Beef and Broccoli Noodle Bowls

This dish serves up tender slices of beef that are packed full of flavor and are incredibly juicy, I know you won't be able to get enough of it. It is so delicious I guarantee you will be begging for more.

Makes: 4 to 6 Servings

Total Prep Time: 25 Minutes

Ingredients:

- 6 to 8 Ounces of Ramen Noodles, Fully Cooked

Ingredients For Your Beef Marinade:

- 1 Pound of Flank Steak, Cut Into Thin Sized Pieces
- 2 Tbsp. of Soy Sauce, Low in Sodium
- 1 Tbsp. of Cornstarch
- ½ tsp. of Sriracha
- 1 ½ tsp. of Brown Sugar, Light and Packed

Ingredients For Your Sauce:

- 1 Tbsp. of Sherry, Dry Variety
- ¾ Cup of Water, Warm
- 5 Tbsp. of Oyster Sauce
- 3 Tbsp. of Brown Sugar, Light and Packed
- 4 tsp. of Cornstarch
- ½ tsp. of Salt, For Taste
- ¼ tsp. of Pepper, For Taste

Ingredients For Your Stir Fry:

- 1 Tbsp. of Oil, Peanut Variety
- 1 tsp. of Oil, Sesame Variety
- 3 ½ to 4 Cups of Broccoli, Cut Into Florets
- ¼ Cup of Water, Warm
- 1 Red Bell Pepper, Finely Chopped
- 6 Cloves of Garlic, Minced
- 1 Tbsp. of Ginger, Minced
- 1 Shallot, Finely Chopped
- 1 Cup of Snow Peas, Ends Trimmed

Ingredients For Garnish:

- Some Green Onions, Optional
- Some Sesame Seeds, Lightly Toasted

Directions:

1. First pour all of your ingredients for your marinade into a large sized freezer bag and mix well to combine. Add your beef into your marinade and toss to coat. Place into your fridge to marinate for the next 2 to 8 hours.

2. Then whisk together all of your ingredients for your sauce into a small sized bowl and set aside for later use.

3. Next heat up some oil in a large sized skillet placed over high heat. Once your oil is hot enough add in your beef and cook until thoroughly brown in color. Remove and transfer to a large sized serving plate.

4. Add a spoonful of your peanut oil into your skillet and add in your broccoli. Cook for at least 30 seconds before adding in your water. Cover and reduce the heat to medium. Allow to steam for the next 2 minutes.

5. Push your broccoli to the sides of your skillet and add in some more sesame oil. Once the oil is hot enough add in your red peppers, shallots, minced garlic and grated ginger. Cook for at least one minute.

6. Return your beef back into your skillet along with your snow peas. Toss to combine and add your sauce into your skillet. Cook until your sauce is thick in consistency. This should take at least 1 to 2 minutes.

7. Add in your noodles and toss to combine. Cook until piping hot.

8. Remove from heat and serve with your green onions and sesame seeds if you wish. Enjoy.

Cheesy Italian Baked Ramen Noodles

If you are a huge fan of mac and cheese or baked ziti, then this is one dish you need to try for yourself. It is smothered in cheese and packed full of an Italian flavor I know you won't be able to resist.

Makes: 5 Servings

Total Prep Time: 18 Minutes

Ingredients:

- 3 Packs of Ramen Noodles, Plain Variety
- 2 Cups of Spaghetti Sauce, Chunky Variety
- 1 ½ Cup of Cheddar Cheese, Freshly Shredded
- Some Sour Cream, Optional

Directions:

1. The first thing that you will want to do is break up your ramen noodles and remove the seasoning packets.

2. Then preheat your oven to 350 degrees.

3. While your oven is heating up place your noodles into a large sized pot filled with water and boil until soft to the touch. Once soft drain your noodles.

4. Place your cooked noodles into a large sized skillet and add in your spaghetti sauce. Stir well to combine and allow to sit for at least one minute.

5. Pour your noodle mixture into a large sized generously greased baking dish.

6. Sprinkle your cheese over the top.

7. Place into your oven to bake for the next 10 to 12 minutes.

8. Remove and allow to cool slightly and serve with your sour cream if you wish. Enjoy.

Simple Sesame Noodles

This is an easy sesame noodle recipe that you can make in just under 15 minutes. Feel free to serve this dish warm or cold. Either way I know you are going to love it.

Makes: 4 to 6 Servings

Total Prep Time: 20 Minutes

Ingredients:

- 1 Pound of Spaghetti, Whole Wheat Variety
- ¼ Cup of Soy Sauce, Your Favorite Kind
- 3 Cloves of Garlic, Minced
- 2 Tbsp. of Ginger, Freshly Grated
- 2 Tbsp. of Vinegar, Rice Variety
- 1 Tbsp. of Oil, Sesame Variety
- 1 tsp. of Oil, Canola Variety
- ½ tsp. of Sriracha
- ½ Cup of Green Onions, Thinly Sliced
- Some Sesame Seeds, Lightly Toasted and For Garnish
- Some Green Onions, Thinly Sliced

Directions:

1. The first thing that you will want to do is cook your pasta according to the directions on the package until tender to the touch. Once tender, drain and set aside for later use.

2. Then use a medium sized bowl and add in your favorite soy sauce, ginger, minced garlic, vinegar, both types of oils and Sriracha sauce. Whisk thoroughly until evenly combined.

3. Add your pasta to this bowl and toss to combine. Add in your green onions and toss again to combine.

4 Serve with your green onions and sesame seeds for garnish.

Taco Style Ramen Bowls

If you are on a tight budget or only have a couple of bucks to spend, then this is the perfect dish for you to make. This dish is full of spice and flavor, making it the perfect dish to satisfy all of your ramen noodle cravings.

Makes: 2 Servings

Total Prep Time: 15 Minutes

Ingredients:

- 1 Pack of Ramen Noodles, Beef Flavored
- 1, 15 Ounce Can of Tomatoes, Fire Roasted Variety and Finely Diced
- ½ Cup of Water, Warm
- 2 Tbsp. of Taco Seasoning
- ½ Cup of Chicken, Canned and Finely Shredded
- ½ Cup of Corn, Frozen, Honey Roasted and Sweet Variety
- ½ Cup of Cheddar Cheese, Finely Shredded
- ¼ Cup of Cilantro

Directions:

1. Use a large sized pot of water to a boil and add in your ramen noodles along with half of your seasoning packed.

2. Add in your tomatoes and bring this mixture to a boil. Cook until your noodles are soft to the touch. This should take at least 3 minutes.

3. Remove from heat and pour into your serving bowl.

4. Sprinkle your remaining beef seasoning over your shredded chicken and place on top of your cooked ramen.

5. Heat up your corn in your microwave until piping hot. Place on top of your corn and top off with your cheese and cilantro. Serve while still hot and enjoy.

Pot Sticker Noodle Bowls

This is a great tasting ramen recipe to make if you are looking for a healthy gluten free alternative to take out. Easy to make in just under 30 minutes, this is one dish I know you are going to want to make over and over again.

Makes: 5 Servings

Total Prep Time: 25 Minutes

Ingredients:

- 8 ounces of Noodles, Rice Variety and Gluten Free
- ½ Cup + 3 Tbsp. of Soy Sauce, Your Favorite Kind
- ¼ Cup of Chicken Broth, Gluten Free and Homemade Preferable
- 2 tsp. of Vinegar, Rice Variety
- ½ tsp. of Ginger, Freshly Grated
- Dash of Red Chili Flakes
- 2 Eggs, Large in Size and Beaten lightly
- 1 Tbsp. of Oil, Canola Variety
- 1 Pound of Pork, Lean and Ground
- Dash of White Pepper, For Taste
- 1, 14 Ounce Bag of Coleslaw Mix, Fresh
- 7 Green Onions, Chopped Into Small Sized Pieces
- 2 Cloves of Garlic, Minced

Directions:

1. The first thing that you will want to do is prepare your noodles according to the directions on the package.

2. Next use a small sized bowl and add in your soy sauce, homemade chicken broth, vinegar, grated ginger and pepper flakes. Stir until thoroughly combine.

3. Whisk your eggs in a separate small sized bowl and set aside for later use.

4. Next heat up a large sized wok and add in some oil over high heat. Once it is hot enough add in your pork and season with a dash of white pepper. Cook until brown in color and fully cooked through.

5. Add in your coleslaw mix and green onions. Cook until your coleslaw begins to wilt. This should take at least 1 minute. Then add in your garlic and continue to cook for an additional 30 seconds.

6. Make a well in the center of your mixture and add in your beaten eggs. Toss thoroughly to combine and continue to cook until your eggs are set.

7. Add in your cooked noodles and continue to cook for the next 5 minutes.

8. Remove from heat and serve right away.

Beef Pho Noodle Soup

Here is another deliciously simple dinner recipe that you can make any day of the week. It is loaded with filling beef, rice noodles and healthy bean sprouts. This dish will leave you feeling full and satisfied for many hours to come.

Makes: 4 to 6 Servings

Total Prep Time: 16 Minutes

Ingredients For Your Beef Broth:

- 64 Ounces of Beef Broth, Organic Variety
- 5 Star of Anise
- 1 Stick of Cinnamon, Fresh
- 2 Cups of Noodles, Rice Variety

Ingredients For Your Beef:

- ½ Pound of Sirloin Steak, Cut Into Paper Thin Slices
- Dash of Salt and Pepper, For Taste

Ingredients For Your Toppings:

- 1 to 2 Jalapeno Peppers, Thinly Sliced
- 1 Cup of Bean Sprouts, Fresh
- 1 Bunch of Cilantro, Fresh and Roughly Chopped
- 1 Lime, Large in Size and Cut Into Wedges
- 1 to 2 Stalks of Scallions, Trimmed and Finely Diced
- 1 Avocado, Large in Size, Peeled, Seeded and Thinly Sliced
- Some Tsang Fry Classic Sauce
- Some Tsang Szechuan Spicy Sauce

Directions:

1. Add your beef stock, anise and cinnamon stick to a large sized stock pot. Set over low heat and bring to a simmer.

2. Next cook your rice noodles according to the directions on the package.

3. Remove your anise and cinnamon from your stock and spoon into your serving bowls.

4. Top off with your noodles, sliced beef, and desired toppings. Drizzle your choice of sauce over the top and enjoy right away.

Conclusion

Well, there you have it!

Hopefully by the end of this book you have learned how to cook some of the most delicious ramen noodle dishes that I know your friends and family are going to fall in love with. Regardless if you are on a tight budget or whether you are looking for a classy meal to serve for your significant other, I hope that you are able to do so with the 25 delicious recipes inside of this book.

So, what is the next step for you?

The next step for you to take is to begin making all of the recipes you have found in this book. Once you have done that I highly recommend trying your hand at making your own ramen noodle recipes from scratch using some of your favorite ingredients.

Good luck!

Author's Afterthoughts

Thanks ever so much to each of my cherished readers for investing the time to read this book!

I know you could have picked from many other books but you chose this one. So a big thanks for downloading this book and reading all the way to the end.

If you enjoyed this book or received value from it, I'd like to ask you for a favor. Please take a few minutes to post an honest and heartfelt review on Amazon.com. Your support does make a difference and helps to benefit other people.

Thanks for your Reviews!

Rachael Rayner

About The Author

Rachael Rayner

Are you tired of cooking the same types of dishes over and over again? As a mother of not one, but two sets of twins, preparing meals became very challenging, very early on. Not only was it difficult to get enough time in the kitchen to prepare anything other than fried eggs, but I was constantly trying to please 4 little hungry mouths under 5 years old. Of course I would not trade my angels for anything in the world, but I had just about given up on cooking, when I had a genius idea one afternoon while I was napping beside one of my sons. I am so happy and proud to tell you that since then, my kitchen has become my sanctuary and my children have become my helpers. I have transformed my meal preparation, my grocery shopping habits, and my cooking style. I am Racheal Rayner, and I am proud to tell you that I am no longer the boring mom sous-chef people avoid. I am the house in our neighborhood where every kid (and parent) wants to come for dinner.

I was raised Jewish in a very traditional household, and I was not allowed in the kitchen that much. My mother cooked the same recipes day in day out, and salt and pepper were probably the extent of the seasonings we were able to detect in the dishes she made. We did not even know any better until we moved out of the house. My husband, Frank is a foodie. I thought I was too, until I met him. I mean I love food, but who doesn't right? He revolutionized my knowledge about cooking. He used to take over in the kitchen, because after all, we were a modern couple and both of us worked full time jobs. He prepared chilies, soups, chicken casseroles—one more delicious than the last. When I got pregnant with my first set of twins and had to stay home on bed rest, I took over the kitchen and it was a disaster. I tried so hard to find the right ingredients and recipes to make the dishes taste something close to my husband's. However, I hated follow recipes. You don't tell a pregnant woman that her food tastes bad, so Frank and I reluctantly ate the dishes I prepared on week days. Fortunately, he was the weekend chef.

After the birth of my first set of twins, I was too busy to even attempt to cook. Sure, I prepared thousands of bottles of milk and purees, but Frank and I ended up eating take out 4 days out of 5. Then, no break for this mom, I gave birth to my second set of twins only 19 months later! I knew that now it was not just about Frank and I anymore, but it was about these little ones for whom I wanted to cook healthy meals, and I had to learn how to cook.

One afternoon in March, when I got up from that power nap with my boys, I had figured out what I needed to do to improve my cooking skills and stop torturing my family with my bland dishes. I had to let go of everything I had learned, tasted, or seen from my childhood and start over. I spent a week organizing my kitchen, and I equipped myself a new blender. I also got some fun shaped cookie cutters, a rolling pin, wooden spatulas, mixing bowls, fruit cutters, and plenty of plastic storage containers. I was ready.

My oldest twins, Isabella and Sophia are now teenagers, and love to cook with their Mom when they are not too busy talking on the phone. My youngest twins Erick and John, are now 10 years old and so helpful in the kitchen, especially when it's time to make cookies.

Let me start sharing my tips, recipes, and shopping suggestions with you ladies and gentlemen. I did not reinvent the wheel here but I did make my kitchen my own, started storing my favorite baking ingredients, and visiting the fresh produce market more often. I have mastered the principles of slow cooking and chopping veggies ahead of time. I have even embraced the involvement of my little ones in the kitchen with me.

I never want to hear you say that you are too busy to cook some delicious and healthy dishes, because BUSY, is my middle name.

Printed in Great Britain
by Amazon